A *flavour* of
KYLEMORE ABBEY

First published in 2018 by

23 Merrion Square North, Dublin 2

www.columbabooks.com

Text copyright © Kylemore Abbey 2018

Photo copyright © Valerie O'Sullivan 2018

All rights reserved. Without limiting the rights under copyright reserved alone, no part of this publication may be reproduced, stored in or introduced into a retrieval system, or transmitted, in any form or by any means (electronic, mechanical, photocopying, recording or otherwise) without the prior written permission of both the copyright owner and the above publisher of the book.

ISBN: 978-1-78218-333-4

Cover and book design by Alba Esteban | Columba Books

Editor Siobhan Prendergast, Dingle Publishing Services

Compiled by Marguerite Foyle, Manager, Mitchell's Café at Kylemore Abbey

Printed by Jellyfish Solutions

A *flavour* of KYLEMORE ABBEY

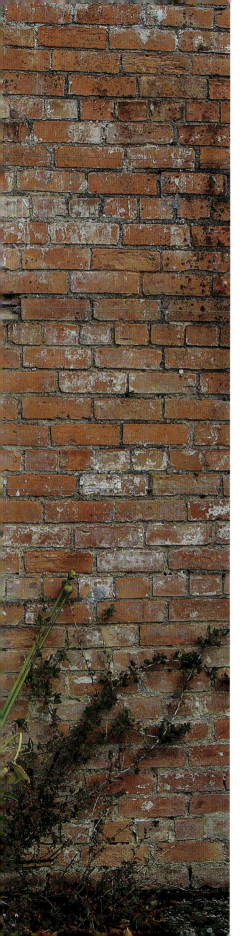

CONTENTS

INTRODUCTION	9
KYLEMORE ABBEY COMMUNITY	13
KYLEMORE ABBEY VICTORIAN WALLED GARDEN	21
CHURCH, MAUSOLEUM AND WALKS	35
SAVOURY RECIPIES	45
SWEET RECIPES	85
CHRISTMAS RECIPES	121

SAVOURY RECIPES INDEX

- Our Traditional Beef Stew 46
- Caramelised Shallot and Guinness Lamb Navarin 47
- Carrot and Coconut Soup 48
- Potato and Dill Soup 49
- Cauliflower and Broccoli Soup 50
- Tomato and Roasted Red Pepper Soup 51
- Tomato and Basil Soup 52
- Honey Roast Bacon and Cabbage Soup 53
- Spiced Beef 54
- Connemara Lamb Burgers 54
- Connemara Lamb Meatballs 55
- Baked Ham 56
- Herb Roast Chicken 58
- Haddock Pie with Mashed Potatoes 59
- Salmon and Spinach Quiche 60
- Killary Fjord Mussels with Sea Spaghetti 62
- Mitchell's Café Chowder 63
- Trout Fillets in White Wine stuffed with Spinach and Nutmeg 64
- Baked Cod stuffed with Smoked Salmon and Horseradish with a Parmesan Crust 66
- Caper Salsa 67
- Smoked Mackerel Pâté 67
- Beetroot & Cabbage Slaw with Greek Lemon Yoghurt 68
- Cucumber Pickle 68
- Hotslaw 69
- Five Bean Salad 71
- Fennel and Orange Salad 72
- Potato Salad with Horseradish and Crème Fraîche 73
- John's Ranch Dressing 74
- Honey and Mustard Dressing 75
- Traditional Brown Bread 76
- Brown Bread made with Fresh Milk 78
- Cajun Chicken Wraps 79
- Cheese Scones 81
- Onion and Poppy Seed Baps 82

SWEET RECIPES INDEX

- Sweet Pastry 86
- Choux Pastry 87
- Shortbread 88
- Orange and Almond Cake with Orange Syrup 89
- Kylemore Apple Tart 90
- Apple Tart with Walnut Crumble Topping 90
- Oatie Biscuits 93
- Kylemore Digestive Biscuits 93
- Easter Simnel Cake 95
- Summer Berry Tart 96
- Lemon Bakewell Tart 98
- Kylemore Chocolate Brownies 100
- Tea Brack 101
- Lemon Meringue Tart 102
- Strawberry Jam 103
- Raspberry and White Chocolate Cheesecake 104
- Apple Jelly 106
- Strawberry and Rhubarb Crumble 107
- Boiled Fruit Cake 109
- Gooseberry Jam 110
- Farmhouse Fruit Cake 111
- Rocky Road 112
- Peach Tray Bake 114
- Spiced Apple and Walnut Bread 115
- Banana and Walnut Bread 116
- Sweet Guinness Bread 117
- Sr Karol's Scones 118

CHRISTMAS RECIPES INDEX

- Kylemore Christmas Cake 124
- Royal Icing 125
- Christmas Mincemeat 126
- Kylemore Liqueur Cream Custard 126
- Kylemore Abbey Christmas Pudding 128
- Frangipane Mince Pies 130

INTRODUCTION

Ora et Labora

The preparation and sharing of food is a precious experience to be savoured and cherished; the fact that it is a daily undertaking does not detract from the singular character of each meal. Nutritious wholesome food shared over a sit-down meal is one of the most enjoyable ways to build and cement relationships. In our Benedictine community in Kylemore, we respect the gift of good food and dedicate a time to share our food. Whatever your circumstances and wherever you are, we hope you will enjoy and savour the recipes we have lovingly compiled with our hardworking staff who run our kitchen and restaurant.

This book presents a mouth-watering selection of traditional and contemporary recipes. There are world-renowned favourites such as our Connemara Lamb Stew and Traditional Apple Pie, and also less well known, but no less delicious, recipes such as Salmon and Spinach Quiche, Fennel and Orange salad, as well as our Strawberry Cheesecake. We like to use fresh produce – and are fortunate to have our Victorian Walled Garden supply us with vegetables, fruits and salads – so do try to source fresh produce when possible or better still, grow your own.

It is our hope that you will savour the fruits of our *Ora et Labora* (Pray and Work) which is the guiding spirit of the Benedictine community.

Built as a breathtaking castle in 1868 by Mitchell Henry for his wife Margaret, Kylemore Abbey is home to a Benedictine Community of nuns, who arrived at Kylemore in 1920 after their abbey in Ypres, Belgium was destroyed in the early months of World War I. Settling at Kylemore, the Benedictine Community opened a world-renowned boarding school for girls and began restoring the Abbey, Gothic Church and Victorian Walled Garden to their former glory.

The smoke and fragance of incense rise like prayer in the Monastic Church during services.

KYLEMORE ABBEY COMMUNITY

A flavour of KYLEMORE ABBEY

The Benedictine nuns gather for Vespers at the Abbey: (from left) Mother Abbess Máire Hickey, Sr Karol, Sr Genevieve, Sr Magdalena, Sr Aidan, Sr Sheila and Sr Dorothy.

A CALL TO PRAYER...

Following the Reformation, the Catholic faith in the British Isles, including Ireland, was persecuted and suppressed. King Henry VIII aimed to destroy the power of the Anglo-Norman kings and take control of Ireland. He placed English lords in charge of confiscated land and plundered Catholic monasteries and churches. In 1536, Henry was declared head of the Church in Ireland through an act of the Irish parliament. British Catholics left England and opened religious houses abroad. A number of monasteries originated from one such Benedictine house founded by Lady Mary Percy in Brussels in 1598, including one in Ghent, Belgium, now St. Mary's Abbey, Oulton, Staffordshire, England. Ghent, in turn, founded several Benedictine houses, one of which was at Ypres in Belgium where the nuns became known as the "Irish Dames of Ypres". It was there that many daughters of Irish nobility were educated. The Benedictine community left Ypres after the Abbey was destroyed in the early days of World War I. The Community first took refuge in England and later in Co. Wexford, before eventually settling in Kylemore in December 1920.

At Kylemore, the nuns opened an international boarding school for girls and established a day school for local girls. In addition to the school, they ran a farm and guesthouse. Sadly, a devastating fire in 1959 caused the closure of the guesthouse. Kylemore Abbey School closed in 2010 and the nuns have since been developing retreat activities together with new educational and crafts initiatives.

A flavour of KYLEMORE ABBEY

Interior, Monastic Church at Kylemore (former School Gymnasium).

KYLEMORE ABBEY COMMUNITY

" Listen carefully to the Master's instructions, and attend to them with the ear of your heart. "

Rule of St Benedict: Prologue 1

A flavour of KYLEMORE ABBEY

Sr Genevieve, Kylemore Abbey's Chocolatier.

KYLEMORE ABBEY COMMUNITY

The Benedictines have a tradition spanning 1,500 years of producing high-end, labour intensive produce. World-renowned are their breweries, especially in Europe, where nuns and monks still retain some of the oldest and best recipes in the world. Other skills associated with monasteries are the art of baking, making preserves, card production, farming, bookbinding and making soaps.

Following the closure of Kylemore Abbey's school in 2010, the Home Economics room was converted into a chocolate kitchen and Sr. Genevieve trained with a Chocolatier. The award-winning Kylemore chocolate brand is renowned for its high-quality, rich dark and milk chocolate in bars, honeycomb, macaroons and luxurious individual chocolates, all made with a blend of French Valrohna chocolate.

Sr. Genevieve and her team were delighted to receive their first Blas na hÉireann Irish Taste Award Gold Medal in 2015.

Kylemore Abbey Victorian Walled Garden

The serenity and order of Kylemore's Victorian Walled Garden in the most untamed of landscapes in Connemara is unexpected to say the least. It is here, where majestic mountains rise all around, bogs give way to old wooded areas and the wild, ancient beauty of Connemara has remained unchanged for centuries, that Mitchell Henry built his castle. He also created the remarkable six-acre walled garden using a workforce of some forty gardeners, and the fact that it was in the middle of a bog – the only garden of its kind in Ireland to be located in a bog – did not deter him!

Mitchell Henry used advanced initiatives throughout the garden. The 21 glasshouses, for example, were heated by three boilers (one of which doubled as a lime kiln) and a complex system of underground hot-water pipes measuring over 1,500 meters in length. It was in the lime kiln, which still exists, in the heart of the garden buildings, that limestone was heated to high temperature to produce quicklime. The quicklime was then spread on the land to break up heavy soil, neutralising the highly acidic boggy soil. The garden was so advanced for its time that it was compared in magnificence with that of Kew Gardens in London.

When Mitchell Henry sold the estate the garden fell into decline and, as the years passed, became completely overgrown, all traces of its former glory hidden from view. In 1995 the Benedictine nuns, led by Sr Magdalena, began an extensive, painstaking process of restoration with a small, dedicated team of gardeners. It remains an amazing testament to their dedication, that the garden was opened to public in 2000 and was awarded the prestigious Europa Nostra Award in 2001.

The heritage garden, displaying only plant varieties from the Victorian era, is divided into two distinct parts by a beautiful, clear mountain stream. In the eastern half is the formal flower garden, glasshouses, the head gardener's house and the garden bothy – where the gardeners would have lived many years ago. The western part of the garden includes a vegetable garden, herbaceous border, fruit trees, rockery and herb garden. Beyond the west gate of the garden there is a plantation of young oak trees which, in years to come, will be replanted throughout the estate.

KYLEMORE ABBEY VICTORIAN WALLED GARDEN

Map of Victorian Walled Garden

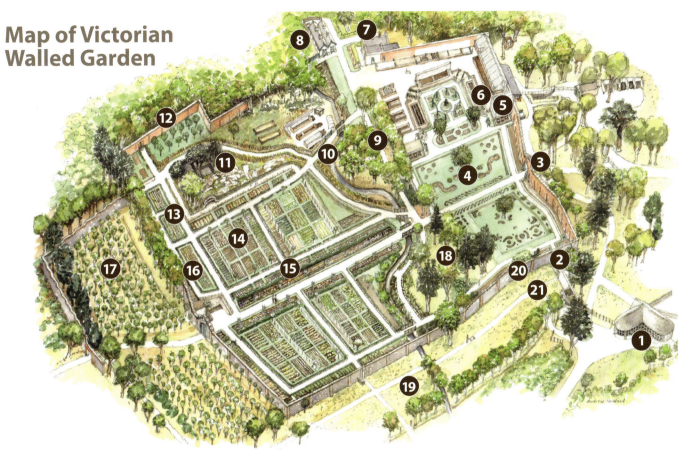

Map Legend:
1. Tea House
2. Garden Entrance
3. Main Gate
4. Formal Flower Garden
5. Lime Kiln
6. Glasshouses
7. Bothy
8. Head Gardener's House
9. Woodland
10. Stream
11. Rockery
12. Nuttery
13. Herb Garden
14. Kitchen Garden
15. Herbaceous Border
16. Cut Flowers
17. Tree Sponsorship Area
18. Fernery
19. Wild Garden Walk
20. Shrub Border
21. Pigsty

A flavour of KYLEMORE ABBEY

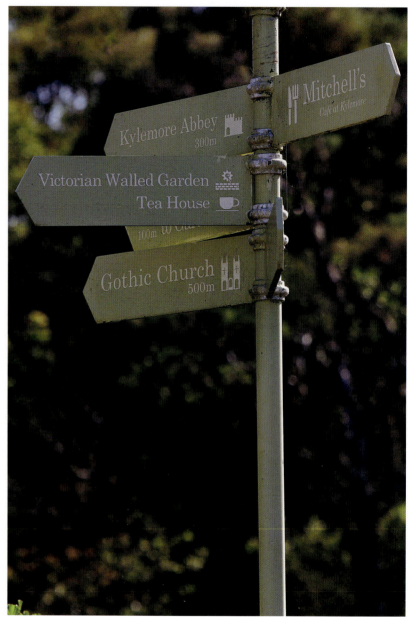

KYLEMORE ABBEY VICTORIAN WALLED GARDEN

Head Gardener's House.

A flavour of KYLEMORE ABBEY

Garden tool shed.

KYLEMORE ABBEY VICTORIAN WALLED GARDEN

A flavour of KYLEMORE ABBEY

Kylemore Abbey Victorian Walled Garden

A flavour of KYLEMORE ABBEY

KYLEMORE ABBEY VICTORIAN WALLED GARDEN

A flavour of KYLEMORE ABBEY

Kylemore Abbey Victorian Walled Garden

CHURCH, MAUSOLEUM AND WALKS

A flavour of KYLEMORE ABBEY

CHURCH, MAUSOLEUM AND WALKS

Along the shores of Lough Pollacappul stands the neo-Gothic Church at Kylemore. Built in the style of a 14th-century miniature cathedral, this elegant building is a lasting testament to the love of Mitchell Henry for his wife, Margaret. In 1874, while the Henry family holidayed in Egypt, tragedy struck on the River Nile. Margaret contracted a fever and died sixteen days later. A heartbroken Mitchell Henry built the little church on the grounds of Kylemore in her memory. The church has many feminine shapes and details; angels instead of gargoyles, floral motifs in the stonework and elegant multi-coloured marble pilasters. Having been unused for many years, the church has been restored by the Benedictine community and, as well as providing a space for quiet prayer and reflection, the building provides wonderful acoustics for musical recitals, poetry readings and community celebrations.

A flavour of KYLEMORE ABBEY

The exterior and interior of the neo-gothic church.

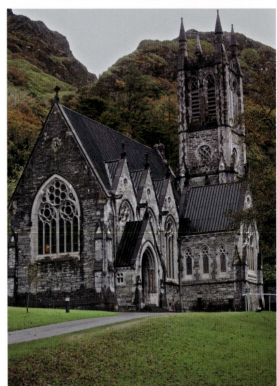

CHURCH, MAUSOLEUM AND WALKS

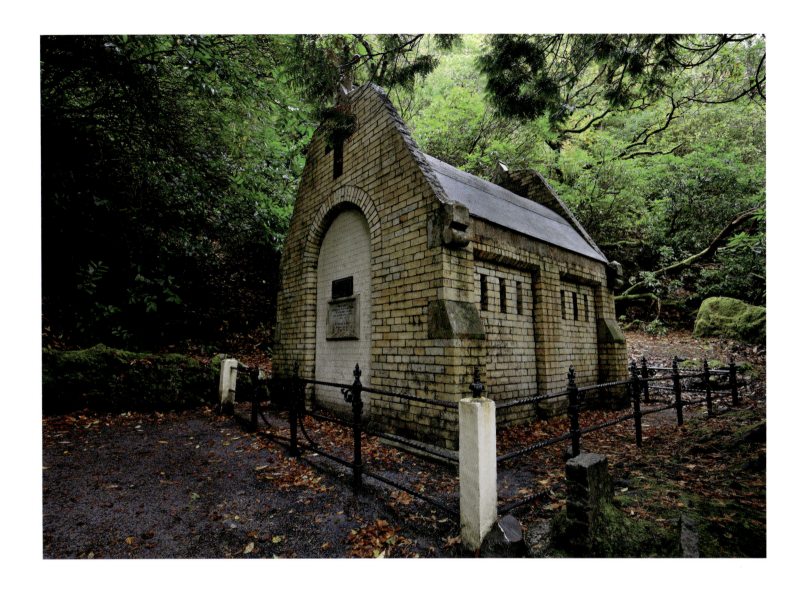

The Mausoleum of Mitchell and Margaret Henry

When Margaret Henry died on a family holiday in Egypt in 1874, her body was embalmed for the return journey to Ireland and was placed in the little mausoleum in the woods.

Following his death in London in 1920, Mitchell Henry's remains were also interred there.

A flavour of KYLEMORE ABBEY

CHURCH, MAUSOLEUM AND WALKS

Kylemore Abbey lakeshore in autumn, set against its ancient oak woods mirrored in Lough Pollacappul.

A flavour of KYLEMORE ABBEY

CHURCH, MAUSOLEUM AND WALKS

Kylemore Abbey Fishery has been in the care of the Benedictine community since they came to Kylemore in 1920. The Fishery consists of the Kylemore, Middle and Castle Lakes along with seven kilometres of the Dawros River which enters the sea in Ballynakill Bay. Having recently undergone a programme of refurbishment, access to all beats has been improved, new boats and engines have been purchased and new pools and walkways have been constructed.

Left: Nigel Rush, Manager, Kylemore Abbey Fishery.

SAVOURY RECIPES

OUR TRADITIONAL BEEF STEW

- 1 KG LEAN BEEF, DICED
- 1 MEDIUM ONION, DICED
- 4 STICKS OF CELERY, CHOPPED
- 4 CLOVES OF GARLIC, FINELY DICED
- 2 LARGE CARROTS, DICED
- 100 ML RAPESEED OIL
- 2 TBSP TOMATO PUREE
- 2.5 L BEEF OR CHICKEN STOCK
- 6 LEAVES OF FRESH BASIL, FINELY CHOPPED
- SEA SALT
- CRACKED BLACK PEPPER

Heat the oil in a large saucepan and in small batches brown the beef and season with salt and pepper; this should take approximately 7 minutes. When the beef is browned off, add the vegetables and sauté for 5 minutes or until vegetables have also browned. Add the tomato puree and sauté for further 3–4 minutes. Add the stock and bring to the boil. Lower the heat to allow the stew to simmer slowly for approximately 90 minutes.

Alternatively you can cook the stew in a covered, ovenproof dish at 160°C for 90 minutes or until the beef is beautifully tender. When the beef is tender, the sauce should also be reduced and thickened. Remove the stew from the heat, stir in the fresh basil and serve with rice or mashed potato.

SAVOURY RECIPES

CARAMELISED SHALLOT AND GUINNESS LAMB NAVARIN

500 G CONNEMARA LAMB, DICED

50 ML RAPESEED OIL

2 TBSP PLAIN FLOUR

500 ML GUINNESS

50 G RAISINS

1 L CHICKEN STOCK

1 CARROT, DICED

1 PARSNIP, DICED

1 COURGETTE, DICED

6 SAGE LEAVES, CHOPPED

200 G SHALLOTS

1 TBSP SUGAR

50 G BUTTER

Heat the oil in a medium saucepan and add the lamb. Keep frying until the lamb is browned all over. Add in the flour and fry again until it is browned. This will look very dry. Slowly add first the Guinness and then the stock. This can now be left simmering on low heat for 1 hour.

Peel the shallots and put them whole in a small pot with the sugar and the butter, and cover with cold water. Simmer the shallots until they are soft enough to fall off a knife when pressed. Take the shallots out and continue simmering and reducing the liquid until it is a light brown thickened caramel. Then add the shallots back in and set aside.

Check the lamb regularly. After 1 hour, add in the carrots, parsnips and raisins. Cook for a further 15 minutes. Once the lamb is tender add in the courgettes and the shallot mixture and cook for another 5 minutes. Finally stir in the sage and let the navarin settle for 5 minutes before serving.

Serve with creamy mashed potatoes.

CHEF'S TIP

Adding Guinness to any stew or casserole gives it a silky, luxurious shine and texture.

CARROT AND COCONUT SOUP

50 G BUTTER

2 MEDIUM ONIONS

3 CLOVES OF GARLIC, PEELED

2 STICKS OF CELERY, ROUGHLY CHOPPED

8 MEDIUM CARROTS, PEELED AND CHOPPED

2 L CHICKEN OR VEGETABLE STOCK

400 ML TIN OF COCONUT CREAM

SALT

BLACK PEPPER

In a large pot, sweat the onion, garlic and celery in the butter on medium heat until softened. Add the chopped carrots and allow to cook for 5 minutes. Pour in the stock and bring to boil. Reduce the heat and leave to simmer for 40 minutes. Add the coconut cream and blend. Season well.

Serve with fresh brown bread.

SAVOURY RECIPES

POTATO AND DILL SOUP

50 G BUTTER

2 MEDIUM ONIONS

10 CLOVES OF GARLIC, PEELED

2 STICKS OF CELERY

6 MEDIUM POTATOES, SLICED

2 TBSP CHOPPED FRESH DILL (SAVE THE STALKS)

2 L CHICKEN OR VEGETABLE STOCK

200 ML CREAM

Roughly chop the onion, garlic and celery and in a large pot and sweat them in the butter on medium heat until softened. Add the potatoes and dill stalks and cook for 5 minutes. Pour in the stock and bring to boil. Reduce the heat and leave to simmer for 40 minutes. Add the cream and the fresh dill before blending.

Delicious served with Kylemore Traditional Brown Bread (page 76).

CHEF'S TIP

If you have no stock available, you can use one jelly stockpot.

CAULIFLOWER AND BROCCOLI SOUP

- 50 G BUTTER
- 2 MEDIUM ONIONS, ROUGHLY CHOPPED
- 3 CLOVES OF GARLIC, PEELED
- 2 STICKS OF CELERY, ROUGHLY CHOPPED
- 6 POTATOES, PEELED AND SLICED
- 2 HEADS OF BROCCOLI, CHOPPED (INCLUDE THE STALKS)
- 1 HEAD OF CAULIFLOWER FLORETS
- 2 L CHICKEN OR VEGETABLE STOCK
- 100 ML CREAM
- SALT AND BLACK PEPPER

In a large pot sweat the onion, garlic and celery in the butter on medium heat until softened without colouring. Add the sliced potatoes and allow to cook for a further 5 minutes. Add in the broccoli and cauliflower before pouring in the stock. Bring to the boil and then reduce the heat and leave to simmer for 40 minutes. Add the cream and blend. Check the seasoning, adding a little salt and pepper if needed.

Serve with fresh brown bread.

SAVOURY RECIPES

TOMATO AND ROASTED RED PEPPER SOUP

50 G BUTTER

1 MEDIUM ONION, DICED

2 CLOVES OF GARLIC, CRUSHED

2 STICKS OF CELERY WITH LEAVES IF POSSIBLE, ROUGHLY CHOPPED

2 CARROTS, ROUGHLY CHOPPED

60 G TOMATO PASTE

4 FRESH TOMATOES, ROUGHLY CHOPPED

200 ML TINNED CHOPPED TOMATOES

150 G ROASTED RED PEPPERS (FRESHLY ROASTED IN YOUR KITCHEN OR JARRED FROM THE SUPERMARKET)

50 G SUGAR

1 L VEGETABLE STOCK

SALT

BLACK PEPPER

Melt the butter in a medium-sized saucepan and add in the onion, garlic, celery and carrots. When the vegetables have sweated off, add the tomato paste and cook for two minutes. Add in the fresh tomatoes, chopped tomatoes, roasted peppers, sugar and vegetable stock. Simmer on low heat for 30–40 minutes, stirring occasionally. Once the vegetables are cooked, blend with a stick blender until smooth. Season well with salt and pepper.

TOMATO AND BASIL SOUP

50 G BUTTER

1 SMALL ONION, DICED

2 CLOVES OF GARLIC, CRUSHED

½ STICK OF CELERY WITH LEAVES IF POSSIBLE

1 CARROT

60 G TOMATO PASTE

6 CHERRY TOMATOES

200 ML TINNED CHOPPED TOMATOES

50 G SUGAR

500 ML VEGETABLE STOCK

100 ML FRESH CREAM

25 G FRESH BASIL, CHOPPED OR 1 TBSP OF DRIED BASIL

SALT AND BLACK PEPPER

Roughly chop the celery, carrot and tomatoes. Melt the butter in a medium sized saucepan and add in the onion, garlic, celery and carrots. If you are using dried basil, add it in now. When the vegetables have sweated off, add the tomato paste and fry for two minutes. Add in the fresh tomatoes, chopped tomatoes, sugar and vegetable stock. Simmer on low heat for 30-40 minutes stirring occasionally.

Once the vegetables are cooked, add in the cream and blend with a stick blender until smooth. If you are using fresh basil add it now. Season with salt and pepper if desired.

SAVOURY RECIPES

Honey Roast Bacon and Cabbage Soup

2 tbsp rapeseed oil

1 medium onion, diced

1 clove of garlic, crushed

1 head of green cabbage, julienne

4 tbsp honey

1½ l chicken stock

1 tsp ground cloves

4 sprigs of fresh parsley, finely chopped (stalks chopped separately)

2 large potatoes

100 ml cream

100 g diced roast ham

Heat the oil in a large pot. Add in garlic, onion, potatoes and parsley stalks. Sweat until soft with no colour, approx. 4 minutes. Stir in honey, ground cloves and cabbage. Sweat for 2 minutes. Add in chicken stock and allow to cook for 20 minutes. Blend with a hand blender (we sieve the soup after blending to achieve a smoother texture). Stir in cream, chopped ham and parsley.

Serve with a sprinkling of fresh parsley and some freshly baked brown bread.

This is a take on a traditional Irish dinner in a bowl!

We grow a Victorian Parsley called Italian Giant in our 6-acre walled garden.

SPICED BEEF

- 6 LB BEEF, TOPSIDE
- 6 BAY LEAVES, CHOPPED
- 2 TSP GROUND CLOVES
- 12 GARLIC CLOVES, CRUSHED
- 4 TSP MIXED SPICE
- 8 TSP SEA SALT
- 3 TSP CRUSHED BLACK PEPPERCORNS
- 6 TABLESPOONS BROWN SUGAR
- 4 TABLESPOONS TREACLE
- 2 TABLESPOONS GROUND NUTMEG
- 1 TSP CINNAMON
- 3 TSP CHILLI POWDER
- 1 BOTTLE OF GUINNESS

Put all of the ingredients except the beef and the Guinness into a blender and blend to form a paste. Rub the paste into the meat, cover and refrigerate. Continue to rub the mixture into the beef once or twice a day for a week. Turn the beef as you repeat the process. The spices and flavourings will mix with the juices drawn from the beef.

Add a bottle of Guinness to cold water in a large pot and add the beef. Bring to boil before simmering gently for 6 hours. Turn off the heat and allow the beef to cool in the cooking liquid. When cool remove the beef from the liquid and place on a serving dish. Cover with a weighted plate. Refrigerate until serving.

Serve cold and thinly sliced

CONNEMARA LAMB BURGERS

- 450 G LEAN LAMB MINCE
- 45 G FRESH BREADCRUMBS
- 1 TBSP GRAINY MUSTARD
- 1 SMALL RED ONION, FINELY CHOPPED
- SMALL AMOUNT OF FRESHLY CHOPPED MINT
- SALT AND PEPPER
- 1 EGG
- (1 TBSP CHILLI JAM FOR A FIERY BURGER)

In a bowl stir to combine the mince, breadcrumbs, mustard, onion, mint, salt and pepper. Add the egg, mix and shape into 4 large burgers or 6 smaller burgers. Chill for 20 minutes before cooking.

Heat 2 tbsp oil in a pan and cook for 6-7 minutes each side.

CONNEMARA LAMB MEATBALLS

1 KG LAMB MINCE

1 CARROT

1 ONION

3 CLOVES OF GARLIC

2 STICKS OF CELERY

4 SPRIGS FRESH ROSEMARY

10 CREAM CRACKERS

1 TSP SEA SALT

½ TSP CRACKED BLACK PEPPER

2 EGGS

100 ML RAPESEED OIL

500 ML PASSATA

2 TINS CHOPPED TOMATOES

2 TBSP CHILLI SAUCE (OPTIONAL)

CHEF'S TIP

This recipe works equally well with beef or pork. You can also use gravy instead of tinned tomatoes and serve with potatoes.

Put the lamb mince in an oversized bowl. Using a food processor or a hand grater, pulse the carrot, onion, garlic, celery and rosemary together and add to the lamb.

Crush the crackers in a zip lock bag using a rolling pin, until they resemble large breadcrumbs. Add this to the lamb along with the sea salt and black pepper. Crack in the eggs and mix everything together with your hands. Wet the palms of your hand with oil to stop the meat sticking to them. Pinch golf ball-sized lumps out of the mixture and gently roll them to form balls. When half of the mixture is used up, start frying the balls in a wide-bottomed pot on high heat with the 100 ml of rapeseed oil covering the bottom of the pot. In batches brown the balls all around and remove them from heat. When the last batch of the balls are in the pot, tip in the passata, tinned tomatoes and chilli sauce (if using). Add the rest of the meat balls back into the pot and bring to boil. Allow to simmer for 30–35 minutes.

Serve with pasta or rice.

BAKED HAM

For the ham

2.5 KG LOIN OF BACON

For the steam tray

HANDFUL OF BLACK PEPPERCORNS

1 ONION, STUDDED WITH CLOVES

1 BAY LEAF

2 STALKS CELERY, ROUGHLY CHOPPED

HANDFUL OF PARSLEY AND STALKS

For glazing

½ JAR APPLE JELLY

1 TBSP ENGLISH MUSTARD

We sometimes use loin of bacon for ease of cutting and serving and because it has a shorter cooking time. Here, at Kylemore, we steam the bacon. The usual cooking times will work – 20 minutes per 450g together with an additional 20 minutes.

Preheat the oven to 160°C.

In your steam tray or oven proof saucepan put in your rinsed piece of bacon, add in onion, pepercorns, bay leaf, celery and parsley. Cover with water, place in the oven and steam to cook according to the weight of the meat. Steam cooking in the oven is a very convenient cooking method as you can set your timer and walk away from it, without any danger of water spilling onto your oven top or the pot boiling dry. Once cooked, as dictated by weight, remove from the water and place in an oven tray. Remove excess fat, score the remaining fat and smear with your glaze, after combining the glaze ingredients. Return to a hot oven and roast at 160°C for 30 minutes until a nice golden colour is achieved.

SAVOURY RECIPES

HERB ROAST CHICKEN

For the chicken

1 LARGE CHICKEN

200 G BUTTER, SOFTENED

1 LEMON, HALVED

1 GARLIC CLOVE, SMASHED

BUNCH OF THYME

SALT AND BLACK PEPPER

Vegetable base

1 YELLOW, RED AND GREEN WHOLE PEPPER

1 BUTTERNUT SQUASH

1 ONION

2 SWEET POTATOES

SUNFLOWER OIL

THYME, SALT AND PEPPER

For the gravy

500 ML VEGETABLE STOCK

HERBS, CHOPPED

1 TBSP CORNFLOUR

Preheat the oven to 160°C. Rub the softened butter over the chicken. Squeeze the lemon over the chicken and then insert it into the cavity with the garlic and the thyme. Season the chicken well with salt and pepper.

Place the vegetables in the bottom of a roasting dish. Toss in the sunflower oil and thyme, season with the salt and pepper. Sit the chicken on top of the prepared vegetables and roast in the oven for 1 hour 15 minutes, depending on weight. Once cooked, remove the chicken from the dish, cover with tin foil to keep warm and to allow the meat to rest. Remove the roasted vegetables and set aside.

To make the gravy, place the roasting dish on a medium heat and pour in 500 ml of vegetable stock. Add in chopped herbs and allow to cook for 5–10 minutes to reduce and thicken. Mix 1 tbsp of cornflour with a tbsp of cold water in a cup, stirring to remove lumps. Whisk into the tray of stock, check for seasoning and reduce to taste. Serve with your carved chicken and roasted vegetables.

SAVOURY RECIPES

Haddock Pie with Mashed Potatoes

For the pie

1 KG SMOKED HADDOCK, SKINNED AND DEBONED

1 SMALL ONION, DICED

SMALL BUNCH OF SAGE, CHOPPED

700 G COOKED POTATOES, MASHED WITH 100G MELTED BUTTER, SALT AND PEPPER

Basic White Sauce

1 ONION, STUDDED WITH 10 WHOLE CLOVES

1 BAY LEAF

HANDFUL OF PARSLEY STALKS

GENEROUS PINCH OF SALT AND WHITE PEPPER

1 L MILK

2 TBSP CORNFLOUR

100 ML MILK OR CREAM

Place the studded onion, bay leaf, parsley stalks, salt and pepper into a saucepan with the milk and bring to boil. Remove from the heat and let rest for about 10 minutes. Meanwhile mix the cornflour with the 100 ml of milk (or cream). Strain the milk and bring back to the boil while adding the cornflour mix to thicken the sauce.

Place the haddock in the bottom of the tray; it can be left whole. Scatter the diced onion on top along with the chopped sage. Add in the white sauce and cover with the mashed potatoes. Spread completely over the top and use a fork to score all over. Bake for 40 mins at 160°C.

SALMON AND SPINACH QUICHE

For the pastry

300 G WHOLEMEAL FLOUR

300 G PLAIN FLOUR

100 G BUTTER, CUBED

150–200 ML WATER

For the filling

250 G SPINACH

600 G SALMON

1 TSP NUTMEG

1 TSP SEA SALT

½ TSP BLACK PEPPER

50 ML OIL

100 ML CREAM

Egg mix

8 EGGS

800 ML CREAM

800 ML MILK

Sieve the plain flour into a bowl, add the wholemeal flour and mix together. Rub in the butter until the mixture resembles breadcrumbs. Add enough water to form a soft paste with the flour when combined. Refrigerate for 1 hour or overnight. Roll out to a thickness of 1 cm and bake blind for 14 minutes at 140°C degrees.

Heat the oil in a saucepan, add the spinach and fry off quickly for 1–2 minutes. Add the nutmeg, sea salt, pepper and cream. Dice the salmon into small cubes. Spread the spinach mix over the pastry base evenly and lay the salmon over the spinach. Season the salmon with the remaining salt and pepper and place your quiche tray in the oven with a baking sheet underneath. Whisk all the egg mix ingredients together and pour over the salmon. Cook for 40 minutes at 160°C degrees.

SAVOURY RECIPES

KILLARY FJORD MUSSELS WITH SEA SPAGHETTI

80 G BUTTER

1 STICK OF LEMON GRASS, CRUSHED

1 LARGE ONION, CHOPPED

5 CLOVES OF GARLIC, CHOPPED

1 SMALL/MEDIUM HEAT CHILLI, CHOPPED

2 KG MUSSELS

250 ML DRY WHITE WINE

50 G DRY SEA SPAGHETTI

1 TABLESPOON RAPESEED OIL

1 BUNCH FRESH CORIANDER

1 LEMON

In a large pot melt the butter and sweat the vegetables over a low heat until cooked but not coloured. Add the mussels and the white wine, and cover with a lid. Allow the mussels to open their shells and release their juices.

In another saucepan steam the sea spaghetti for ten minutes. Heat the oil in a pan and stir fry the spaghetti for 3–4 minutes.

Place the spaghetti on a serving dish and pour the mussels and juice over it. Garnish with some chopped coriander and some lemon wedges.

MITCHELL'S CAFÉ CHOWDER

500 ML FISH STOCK

2 MEDIUM POTATOES, PEELED AND CUBED

20 G DRIED CARRAGEEN

250 ML CREAM

10 G MIXED SEA VEG

300 G FRESHLY SELECTED FISH CHOPPED (WE USE SALMON, COD AND SMOKED HADDOCK)

HANDFUL OF FRESH BASIL, FINELY CHOPPED

Pour the fish stock into a saucepan, add the cubed potatoes and bring slowly to the boil. Once the potatoes are soft, scoop them out with a slotted spoon and set aside. Add in the carrageen and cook for a further 10 minutes before straining to remove the carrageen from the mix. Pour the liquid and potato mix back into your saucepan and add in the cream and sea vegetables. Add in the chopped fish, fresh basil and simmer for 3–4 minutes to cook the fish. Check for seasoning and serve.

CHEF'S TIP

This works well with any kind of fish, and the addition of some blanched vegetables makes for a complete meal. For a richer white sauce you could use half cream and half milk. For an alternative to potatoes try a combination of root vegetables, e.g. carrot, parsnip and sweet potato.

TROUT FILLETS IN WHITE WINE STUFFED WITH SPINACH AND NUTMEG

4 FILLETS OF LAKE TROUT

SEA SALT AND WHITE PEPPER

PINCH OF NUTMEG

2 TBSP RAPESEED OIL

250 G SPINACH

25 G BUTTER

1 ONION, DICED

4 CLOVES OF GARLIC, DICED

1 TSP DILL

4 TBSP WHITE WINE

100 ML CREAM

1 TBSP CORNFLOUR

Skin the trout and pull out all the little pin bones (your fishmonger will do this for you). Season with salt and pepper. Heat the oil in a saucepan over a medium heat and sweat the spinach for a few minutes until wilted, then season with salt, pepper and nutmeg. Remove from the heat and blend the spinach mix. Melt the butter and sweat the onion and garlic in it before adding in the dill and the white wine. Spread the onion mixture onto a baking tray.

Place your trout fillets on top of parchment, cover with the spinach mix and fold over each one. Tie each one into a little parcel and place on the onion mix to cook. Cover the tray with cling film and then tin foil to bake. Bake at 160°C for 12–14 minutes. Once cooked place the trout onto a serving dish and keep warm.

Place baking tray on medium heat. Add the cornflour dissolved into a tablespoon of water into the baking tray with cream and bring the sauce to boil and allow to thicken. Season the sauce to your taste, pour over the trout and serve immediately.

CHEF'S TIP

This dish works for any fish as well as chicken. Just allow more time for the chicken to be thoroughly cooked.

SAVOURY RECIPES

65

BAKED COD STUFFED WITH SMOKED SALMON AND HORSERADISH WITH A PARMESAN CRUST

250 G BREAD, SLIGHTLY STALE

HANDFUL OF FRESH PARSLEY AND DILL, CHOPPED

180 G PARMESAN, FRESHLY GRATED

100 G BUTTER, MELTED

HANDFUL OF SUNDRIED TOMATOES, CHOPPED

SALT AND BLACK PEPPER

1 KG COD, DEBONED AND SKINNED CUT INTO 4 PORTIONS

2 TSP OF HORSERADISH CREAM

4 SLICES OF CONNEMARA SMOKED SALMON

Line baking tray with foil and brush with melted butter. Blitz the bread and parsley in a food processor to fine crumbs, then add the parmesan, melted butter, sundried tomatoes, half a teaspoon of salt and some pepper and blitz again.

Wipe the fish with kitchen paper and cut open along the side to make into two pieces. Lay the bottom piece on the foil, smear with horseradish, place a slice of smoked salmon on top and cover with the second piece of cod. Press the parmesan crumb onto the top of the fish and season with salt and pepper. Cook on a high shelf in the oven for 15 minutes at 180°C until golden brown. Serve with caper salsa (Recipe on opposite page).

SAVOURY RECIPES

CAPER SALSA

50 G CAPERS CHOPPED

2 TOMATOES FINELY DICED, FLESH REMOVED

1 SMALL RED ONION, CHOPPED

1 RED PEPPER, FINELY DICED

8 BASIL LEAVES, FINELY CHOPPED

GLUG OF OLIVE OIL

GLUG OF BALSAMIC VINEGAR

Combine all the ingredients together and leave for 1 hour to allow the flavours to mingle.

SMOKED MACKEREL PÂTÉ

1 PACKET OF LOCAL SMOKED MACKEREL 330 G, SKIN OFF

250 G CREAM CHEESE

ZEST AND JUICE FROM ½ A LEMON

BUNCH OF CHOPPED THYME

2 TBSP OIL FROM SUNDRIED TOMATOES OR OLIVE OIL

BLACK PEPPER TO TASTE

Using a food processor add all the ingredients and whizz to bring to a smooth consistency. Check for seasoning and adjust as required.

Serve with gooseberry preserve.

CHEF'S TIP

This could be used as a starter or as a lunch centre piece with a green salad and some crusty brown bread.

BEETROOT & CABBAGE SLAW WITH GREEK LEMON YOGHURT

250 g cooked beetroot

½ red cabbage

1 red onion

1 green chilli, chopped

small bunch of Flatleaf parsley chopped

200 ml Greek yoghurt

1 lemon, juice and zest

1 garlic clove crushed

1 tsp cumin seeds toasted

salt and black pepper

We grow a huge amount of beetroot in the garden and this is a great way of using it in a salad rather than just on its own.

Peel and grate the beetroot – this is quite messy and it is advisable to wear gloves. Shred the red cabbage and dice the onion. Combine together with parsley and chilli.

In a separate bowl, mix the Greek yoghurt with the lemon juice and zest, garlic, toasted cumin seeds and seasoning. Combine together and pour over the beetroot cabbage mix. Chill for at least 20 minutes for the flavours to mingle.

CUCUMBER PICKLE

1 kg cucumber, thinly sliced

4 small onions, very thinly sliced (we use red and white for colour – red will bleed eventually)

1½ tbsp salt

350 g caster sugar

225 ml white wine vinegar or cider vinegar

small bunch of dill

a few peppercorns

In a large bowl combine the thinly sliced cucumber and the thinly sliced onion. In a separate bowl combine the salt, sugar and vinegar, mixing well to combine. Add the liquid combination to the onion and cucumber. Mix well and sprinkle in the chopped dill and whole peppercorns. Make at least 2 hours ahead of time.

CHEF'S TIP

This will keep in a kilner jar in the fridge for a few days.

HOTSLAW

1 RED CABBAGE, THINLY SLICED

1 RED ONION, THINLY SLICED

1 SMALL RED CHILLI, THINLY SLICED

2 CARROTS, GRATED

50 G FRESH CORIANDER, CHOPPED

Dressing

100 G HONEY

100 ML RED WINE VINEGAR

100 ML RAPESEED OIL

Mix all the vegetables together in a large bowl. Whisk together the honey, vinegar and oil in a separate large bowl until fully mixed. Add the dressing to the vegetables and toss together before serving.

CHEF'S TIP

This salad is better made in advance to let the cabbage absorb the flavour of the dressing.

A flavour of KYLEMORE ABBEY

SAVOURY RECIPES

FIVE BEAN SALAD

250 G EDAMAME BEANS

(CHOOSE FOUR OF THE FOLLOWING BEANS USING COLOUR AS A CHOICE GUIDE)

400 G KIDNEY BEANS

400 G CANNELLINI BEANS

400 G CHICKPEAS

400 G BLACK-EYED BEANS

400 G BLACK BEANS

400 G BUTTER BEANS

1 SMALL TIN OF SWEETCORN, DRAINED

2 RED PEPPERS, CHOPPED SMALL

HONEY AND MUSTARD DRESSING (OPTIONAL)

Steam the edamame beans for 2 minutes and blanch in cold water to refresh. Open all the tins, rinse and drain well. Add all of the beans to a bowl and mix. Add in the sweetcorn and chopped red peppers.

Serve salad with honey and mustard dressing on the side (see page 75).

FENNEL AND ORANGE SALAD

- 2 FENNEL BULBS, FINELY SLICED
- 1 ONION, FINELY SLICED
- 4 ORANGES, CUT INTO SEGMENTS (SAVE THE JUICE LEFT BEHIND FROM SEGMENTING)
- 100 G WALNUTS, CRUSHED
- 3 STICKS OF CELERY, FINELY CHOPPED
- 2 SPRING ONIONS, CHOPPED
- 1 TSP ENGLISH MUSTARD
- 1 TBSP HONEY
- 4 TBSP VINEGAR
- 12 TBSP RAPESEED OIL
- PINCH OF SEA SALT

Toss all the dry ingredients together.

Using a whisk or a blender, whisk together the mustard, honey and vinegar slowly. Add the oil and then the orange juice. Season the dressing with sea salt and toss it into the salad.

CHEF'S TIP

If no fennel is available, you could use kohlrabi or celeriac. We use a Victorian variety of Kohlrabi that is grown in our Victorian Walled Garden.

POTATO SALAD WITH HORSERADISH AND CRÈME FRAÎCHE

900 G BABY POTATOES, HALVED

4 TBSP WHITE WINE VINEGAR

SALT AND PEPPER

300 G PARSNIPS, SHAVED WITH A VEGETABLE PEELER

1 BUNCH OF SCALLIONS, THINLY SLICED

5 TBSP CREAMED HORSERADISH

500 G CRÈME FRAÎCHE

ZEST OF ONE LEMON

SMALL BUNCH OF CHIVES, CHOPPED

Steam the potatoes until cooked and place in a bowl. Add the vinegar, salt, pepper mix and allow to sit for ten minutes to cool. Steam the parsnips for 3–4 minutes and add to the potato mix.

Combine the rest of the ingredients and mix gently into the potatoes and parsnip mix. Taste to check seasoning and adjust if necessary.

CHEF'S TIP

If you do not have creamed horseradish, you could use dry mustard powder for a bit of heat.

JOHN'S RANCH DRESSING

1 L MAYONNAISE

1 TBSP SEAWEED MIX (WE USE IRISH SEAWEED MIX)

¼ L BUTTERMILK

½ TBSP DIJON MUSTARD

¼ TBSP PAPRIKA

¼ TBSP MIXED HERBS

2 CLOVES OF GARLIC, CRUSHED

PINCH BLACK PEPPER

65 ML CIDER VINEGAR

65 G SUGAR

This recipe has been created by Mitchell's Café Head Chef, John O'Toole.

Combine all of the ingredients together and blend to make this delicious dressing, which will keep in your fridge for up to two weeks.

HONEY AND MUSTARD DRESSING

½ L OLIVE OIL

¼ L WHITE WINE VINEGAR

1 TBSP WHOLEGRAIN MUSTARD

225 G HONEY

75 G GARLIC, CRUSHED

½ L SUNFLOWER OIL

SALT AND PEPPER TO TASTE

Put all the ingredients except the oil into a large bowl and blend together using a stick blender. Slowly add the oil continuing to blend. Season to taste. Beautiful served over a fresh green salad.

CHEF'S TIP

This will keep in a sealed jar in the fridge for weeks. Shake before using.

TRADITIONAL BROWN BREAD

Dry ingredients

225 G WHOLEMEAL FLOUR

112 G PLAIN WHITE FLOUR

25 G BRAN

25 G PORRIDGE

1 TSP BREAD SODA

112 G SESAME AND PUMPKIN SEED MIX

Wet ingredients

2 TSP TREACLE

120 ML RAPE SEED OIL

400 ML BUTTERMILK

Mix the dry ingredients together in a bowl, reserving 65 g of the seeds for the top of the loaf. Mix together the wet ingredients before adding them to the dry ingredients and combine. Pour into a greased 2 lb loaf tin, making a slit in the top of the bread to prevent cracking. Sprinkle the seeds over the loaf and bake in a preheated oven for 60 minutes at 170°C or until a skewer comes out clean. Remove from tin and allow to cool on a wire rack.

CHEF'S TIP

This is available as a Kylemore Abbey Baking Mix which can be purchased from our Craft Shop and Mitchell's Café.

SAVOURY RECIPES

BROWN BREAD MADE WITH FRESH MILK

112 G STRONG FLOUR

PINCH OF SALT

1 TSP BREAD SODA

57 G BROWN SUGAR (OPTIONAL)

1 TSP BEXTARTAR

112 G BRAN

225 G WHOLEMEAL FLOUR

2 EGGS

57 G MELTED BUTTER

500 ML FRESH MILK

Sieve the strong flour, salt, bread soda and bextartar together. Add in the bran, sugar and wholemeal flour.

Beat the eggs in a bowl and add the melted butter, before adding both along with the milk to the dry ingredients. Combine and transfer into a greased 2 lb loaf tin. Bake at 180°C for 50 minutes. Transfer onto a wire rack until completely cool.

CAJUN CHICKEN WRAPS

CAJUN MAYONNAISE

PLAIN, SPINACH OR SUNDRIED TOMATO WRAP

CHICKEN, SLICED

STREAKY BACON, GRILLED

RED ONION, SLICED

LETTUCE (OPTIONAL)

We make lots of these daily using plain, spinach or sundried tomato wraps for a variety of flavours. Our dressing is very simply mayonnaise with the addition of cajun spices.

Smear the cajun mayonnaise across the wrap, layer the ingredients in the centre and roll your wrap by folding in the ends first and then folding up to contain the filling.

SAVOURY RECIPES

A flavour of KYLEMORE ABBEY

SAVOURY RECIPES

CHEESE SCONES

500 G SELF-RAISING FLOUR

175 G BUTTER

112 G GRATED CHEDDAR CHEESE

100 G SUNDRIED TOMATOES WITH OIL

1 EGG

¼ L BUTTERMILK

Sieve the flour into a bowl, then rub the butter into the flour until it resembles breadcrumbs. Add the grated cheese and sundried tomatoes along with some of the oil, especially if the tomatoes are marinated in herbs. Add in the egg and the buttermilk and combine into a soft dough. Turn out onto a lightly floured board and knead lightly to smooth over. Roll out with a rolling pin and cut using a cutter. Place on a lightly greased baking sheet and bake for 15 minutes at 170°C until lightly browned.

ONION AND POPPY SEED BAPS

For the filling

1 breast of chicken cooked with cajun spices

¼ red pepper, sliced

¼ yellow pepper, sliced

5 slices of cucumber

1 medium tomato, sliced

mixed lettuce leaves

1 red onion, sliced

For the salad cream

100 ml mayonnaise

1 tsp caster sugar

1 tsp white wine vinegar

a squeeze of fresh lemon juice

pinch of sea veg mix

½ tsp English mustard

Use our cheese scone recipe to make your baps adding 1 tbsp poppy seeds to the recipe and use 2 tbsp of dried onions to decorate the top of them once egg washed. Roll your mix out thinner than the scone and use a larger cutter. Bake as per the scone recipe and allow to cool. Once cooled the baps can be split open and filled.

To make the salad cream simply stir ingredients together until an even blend has been achieved. Smear some of your salad cream across the open sides of the bap and layer on your chicken and salad ingredients.

SAVOURY RECIPES

SWEET RECIPES

SWEET PASTRY

450 G FLOUR

55 G ICING SUGAR

375 G BUTTER OR MARGARINE

1 EGG YOLK

3 TSP LEMON JUICE

COLD WATER TO BIND IF REQUIRED

In a mixing bowl combine the flour, sugar and margarine until the mixture resembles breadcrumbs. Add the egg yolk, lemon juice and combine. Chill for 1 hour before using.

This pastry is used for our apple pies, mince pies and other sweet baking.

CHOUX PASTRY

140 G STRONG FLOUR

½ PINT WATER

112 G BUTTER

¼ TSP VANILLA ESSENCE

4 EGGS BEATEN

To decorate

250 ML CREAM, LIGHTLY WHIPPED

100 G MILK CHOCOLATE

This pastry can be used for éclairs or profiteroles.

Preheat the oven to 160°C.

Sieve the flour onto a plate. Put the water, butter and vanilla essence in a saucepan and melt together until it bubbles. Remove from the heat and allow to cool slightly. Stir in the sieved flour and bring together to form a dough. Using your electric mixer, whisk for a few minutes, adding the eggs gradually until the dough looks shiny. Using a piping bag, pipe out each éclair, approximately 15 cm long, onto a greased tray. Alternatively use two spoons to make profiterole shapes. Cook at 170°C for 40 minutes, then turn out onto a wire rack to cool before filling.

When cool, slit the éclair down the side, fill with whipped cream and pour melted chocolate on top.

A flavour of KYLEMORE ABBEY

SHORTBREAD

250 G FLOUR

150 G BUTTER, SOFTENED

110 G CASTER SUGAR

Preheat the oven 160°C.

Using the paddle/spade attachment on your electric mixer combine all the ingredients in a bowl to form a stiff dough. Cover the dough and chill in the fridge for 30 minutes.

On a floured table roll out the dough thinly and cut into rounds of 50 mm using a scone cutter. Place on a greased baking sheet and bake for 20 minutes at 160°C. Cool on a wire tray.

ORANGE AND ALMOND CAKE WITH ORANGE SYRUP

For the Orange and Almond Cake

3 LARGE WHOLE ORANGES

6 EGGS BEATEN

375 G GROUND ALMONDS

2 TSP GLUTEN-FREE BAKING POWDER

375 G CASTER SUGAR

For the Orange Syrup

500 ML WATER

125 G CASTER SUGAR

JUICE AND ZEST OF ONE ORANGE

1 VANILLA POD

1 STAR ANISE

Preheat the oven to 160°C and line a 23 cm round tin.

Cook the oranges in a saucepan for 40 minutes and then blitz to a smooth paste. Pour the mixture into a bowl, then add in the beaten egg and combine. Fold in the ground almonds, baking powder and caster sugar to form a smooth paste. Pour the mix into the prepared tin and bake for 45 minutes. Turn out onto a baking rack and allow to cool.

To make the orange syrup, place all the ingredients in a saucepan over medium-high heat and bring to the boil. Reduce the heat and simmer until reduced. Allow to cool and serve poured over the cake.

KYLEMORE APPLE TART

For the pastry

375 G FLOUR

30 G ICING SUGAR

225 G BUTTER OR MARGARINE, CUBED

1 TSP LEMON JUICE

1 EGG YOLK

COLD WATER TO BIND IF REQUIRED

For the filling

4 MEDIUM APPLES, PEELED, CORED AND SLICED

75 G CASTER SUGAR

1 EGG YOLK BEATEN

Preheat oven to 160°C. Sieve the flour and icing sugar into a large bowl. Add in the butter and rub into the dry mix until it looks like fine breadcrumbs. Add the lemon juice, egg yolk and gather into one piece by hand and knead lightly.

On a floured table, roll out half of the pastry. Grease a 23 cm tart plate and line with the pastry. Trim the edges with a knife. Spread the apples onto the pastry and evenly sprinkle with sugar. Brush the edges of the pastry with a little water. Roll out the remaining pastry and with it cover the tart. Seal the edges well and flute both edges together with a knife. Brush all over with a little beaten egg yolk and bake in a preheated oven at 160°C for 55 minutes until the pastry is nicely browned. Sprinkle with some caster sugar and serve.

APPLE TART WITH WALNUT CRUMBLE TOPPING

For the crumble mix

175 G FLOUR

1 TSP CINNAMON

110 G BROWN SUGAR

50 G WALNUT CHOPPED

110 G BUTTER

As an alternative to an all-pastry tart we sometimes use this crumble mix as the top layer.

Make your tart as normal; preheat oven to 160°C, line the plate with your prepared pastry, fill with fruit of your choice – apples or rhubarb and strawberry.

To make the walnut crumble sieve the flour into a bowl, add the cinnamon, brown sugar and chopped walnuts and mix. Rub the butter into the mix until it resembles breadcrumbs. Sprinkle the walnut crumble topping over the prepared tart and bake at 180°C for 40 minutes and enjoy

SWEET RECIPES

91

A flavour of KYLEMORE ABBEY

SWEET RECIPES

OATIE BISCUITS

230 G PORRIDGE OATS

90 G CASTER SUGAR

120 G PLAIN FLOUR

PINCH OF SALT

1 TSP BAKING POWDER

230 G BUTTER, MELTED

Preheat the oven to 180°C. Mix all the dry ingredients together and add the melted butter. Bring together and place on a shallow, lined baking tray. Flatten the mixture onto the baking tray and bake at 180°C for 20 minutes. Once cooked cut into squares and leave to cool.

CHEF'S TIP

These biscuits are quick and easy to make, and they leave a lot of room for experimentation. Try adding some chopped nuts or dried fruit into the mix but keep the amount of dry ingredients at the same weight, for example if you are adding in 30 g of chopped nuts, leave out some of the porridge. Adding a squeeze of honey or maple syrup into the mix before baking will give these biscuits a more chewy texture.

KYLEMORE DIGESTIVE BISCUITS

170 G WHOLEMEAL FLOUR

30 G WHITE FLOUR

30 G OATMEAL

2 TSP SUGAR

1 TSP BAKING POWDER

75 G BUTTER

MILK TO BIND

Preheat the oven to 150°C. Mix all the dry ingredients together in a large bowl and rub in the butter. Add enough milk to bind and make into a stiff dough. Turn out onto a floured board and roll out thinly. Cut into rounds using a 50 mm cutter. Put on a greased baking sheet and bake at 150°C for 18–20 minutes. These biscuits should be pale when cooked. Cool on a wire tray.

A flavour of KYLEMORE ABBEY

EASTER SIMNEL CAKE

For the cake

225 G SOFT MARGARINE

225 G LIGHT BROWN SUGAR

4 BEATEN EGGS

225 G SELF-RAISING FLOUR

225 G SULTANAS

225 G CURRANTS

225 G GLACE CHERRIES WASHED AND QUARTERED

225 G CANDIED PEEL CHOPPED

2 LEMONS (GRATED RIND ONLY)

2 LEVEL TSP MIXED SPICE

Filling and topping

450 G ALMOND PASTE

2 TBSP APRICOT JAM

1 EGG BEATEN TO GLAZE

The Simnel Cake is a symbolic Easter cake decorated with eleven marzipan balls around the cake to represent the 11 disciples. Though there were 12 disciples, Judas Iscariot is omitted as he betrayed Jesus.

Preheat the oven to 120°C. Cream the margarine and sugar. Add the beaten eggs and mix. Add the fruit, mixed spice, flour and lemon rind and combine.

Place half the mixture into a 20 cm round cake tin, greased and lined, and level the surface.

Roll one third of the almond paste into a circle the size of the cake tin and place on top of the cake mixture. Spoon the remaining cake mixture on top and level the surface.

Bake in a preheated fan oven at 120°C for 30 minutes or until a skewer comes out clean and the cake is golden brown. Cool in the tin for 30 minutes, before removing the cake from the tin and placing it to cool on a wire rack.

When the cake is cool brush with a little warmed jam. Roll out most of the remaining almond paste to cover the top of the cake, reserving some to roll into 11 balls. Brush the paste and balls with the beaten egg and arrange the almond paste balls around the top of the cake. Cover all but the top of the cake with tinfoil and place in a hot oven for a few minutes to toast.

SUMMER BERRY TART

For the pastry base

100 G BUTTER, CUBED

200 G PLAIN FLOUR

25 G ICING SUGAR, SIFTED

1 EGG, BEATEN

For the cheese filling

450 G SOFT CREAM CHEESE

240 G CASTER SUGAR

2 TSP VANILLA EXTRACT

1 TBSP CREAM

For the fruit topping

6 STRAWBERRIES

12 BLUEBERRIES

6 GRAPES

12 RASPBERRIES

3 ORANGE SEGMENTS

Make the pastry by rubbing the butter into the flour and then add the icing sugar. Stir in the beaten egg to form the dough. Chill for 30 minutes in the fridge.

Preheat the oven to 160°C. Roll out the pastry and fill a 25 cm round tart tin with a loose base. Bake blind using baking beans for 12 minutes at 160°C. Remove baking beans and cook for another 12 minutes until golden brown. Remove from the oven and allow to cool completely.

To make the filling, beat the cheese, caster sugar and vanilla extract together until smooth. Add in the cream and beat until well combined. Fill the pastry base with the cheese filling and smooth out using a palette knife. Leave to chill in the fridge for 20 minutes. Once chilled arrange the fruit on top of the cheese filling.

Make a glaze by microwaving 2 tbsp of apricot jam and 1 tbsp of water for 2 minutes and sieve. Brush the fruit with the glaze.

Serve with freshly whipped cream and sprigs of fresh mint.

CHEF'S TIP

Any fruit you have available will work as a topping for this tart. Use whatever is in season and get creative with the arrangement.

SWEET RECIPES

LEMON BAKEWELL TART

For the sweet pastry

200 G CREAM FLOUR

90 G ICING SUGAR

150 G MARGARINE

3 EGG YOLKS

For the lemon and almond topping mix

110 G BUTTER

110 G CASTER SUGAR

2 EGGS

110 G GROUND ALMONDS

FINELY GRATED ZEST OF 1 LEMON

50 G FLAKED ALMONDS

For the filling

250 G KYLEMORE ABBEY LEMON CURD

Preheat the oven to 150°C

To prepare the pastry mix the flour and sugar together. Rub in the margarine. Slowly add in egg yolks one at a time. Combine to make a smooth pastry. Roll the pastry out on a floured worktop to about 1 cm thickness and line a greased 20 cm pie dish with the pastry.

For the toppings mix cream the butter and sugar together until light and creamy. Beat the eggs and add to the mixture a little at a time. Fold in the almonds and lemon zest.

Spread the lemon curd on the pastry lining your pie dish, leaving about 1 cm from the edge of the dish uncovered. Spread the lemon and almond topping mix evenly all over making sure it reaches the edge of the dish. Sprinkle with flaked almonds. Bake at 150°C for 35–40 minutes or until golden brown.

CHEF'S TIP

Double this pastry recipe and keep half in the freezer as it is a great base for all sorts of tarts and pastries, e.g. apple pie, mince pies.
Replace lemon curd with raspberry jam and leave out the lemon rind from your topping mix to make a traditional bakewell tart.

SWEET RECIPES

CHOCOLATE BROWNIES MADE WITH KYLEMORE CHOCOLATE

225 G BUTTER

225 G KYLEMORE DARK CHOCOLATE
(WE USE THE NUNS' DARK CHOCOLATE 60%)

200 G CASTER SUGAR

2 TSP VANILLA EXTRACT

3 EGGS BEATEN

150 G GROUND ALMONDS

100 G CHOPPED WALNUTS

Preheat the oven to 170°C and line a 24 cm square baking tin.

Gently melt the butter and chocolate in a bowl placed over a saucepan of hot water. Make sure the water cannot get into the bowl. Once melted remove the bowl from the saucepan and add the sugar and vanilla. Allow to cool a little. Beat the eggs into the cooled chocolate mixture and add the almonds and walnuts. Pour into the tin and give a little shake to spread into the tin evenly. Bake in the oven for 25–30 minutes. The top will have set but will have a slight wobble. Once cool, cut carefully into squares.

These are a melting fudgy type brownie with nuts. Served slightly warm with cream or ice cream they are just divine.

SWEET RECIPES

TEA BRACK

- 375 G DRIED FRUIT (WE USE A MIX OF RAISINS, SULTANAS, APRICOTS AND CRANBERRIES)
- 250 ML WARM TEA (YOU HAVE THE OPTION TO USE A FLAVOURED TEA, E.G. EARL GREY)
- 1 LARGE EGG, BEATEN
- 75 G BROWN SUGAR
- 250 G SELF-RAISING FLOUR

Soak the dried fruit and sugar in tea overnight; this allows the fruit to plump up.

Preheat the oven to 160°C and prepare a 2 lb loaf tin lined for baking.

To the fruit and sugar mix add the beaten egg followed by the sieved flour a spoon at a time. If the mix is a little dry, add a little milk. Pour into the prepared tin and smooth over. Cook at 160°C for 1 hour.

CHEF'S TIP

If you wanted to add a little fun to this for Halloween, wrap some coins, as hidden treasure, in greaseproof paper and add to the uncooked mixture before baking.

LEMON MERINGUE TART

For the lemon mix

170 G BUTTER

2 LEMONS, JUICE AND RIND

4 EGGS, SEPARATED AND BEATEN

170 G SUGAR

For the pastry

½ LB SWEET PASTRY, AS PER BAKEWELL TART

Line a 20 cm plate with the pastry and bake blind for 10 minutes at 180°C.

Melt the butter in a saucepan. Add the lemon rind and juice to the butter followed by the whisked egg yolks. Warm through, adding the sugar and stirring all the time. Whisking constantly, continue to cook but do not boil, allowing it to thicken. Once thickened, pour the lemon mix onto the cooked pastry.

Whisk the egg whites in a clean bowl until light and fluffy, and holding in a peak. Spoon or pipe on top of the lemon mix and cook for a further 15 minutes until golden. Allow to sit for 15 minutes before cutting.

CHEF'S TIP

For an alternative filling we use Kylemore Abbey's Lemon Curd.

SWEET RECIPES

STRAWBERRY JAM

2 KG STRAWBERRIES

JUICE OF 2 LEMONS

2 KG SUGAR

Place the strawberries and lemon juice in a saucepan over a low heat with enough water to just cover the base of the saucepan and cook gently. Add in the sugar, stirring to dissolve it and bring to the boil. Once boiled, turn down the heat and simmer gently.

Sterilize 6 jars and lids in the oven for 20 minutes and allow to cool.

Test the jam using the 'saucer test' – put a little jam on a saucer and leave for a few minutes, run your finger over the jam and if you achieve a ripple effect on the jam the setting point has been reached.

Pour into the jars and seal.

RASPBERRY AND WHITE CHOCOLATE CHEESECAKE

For the base

225 g butter melted

400 g digestive biscuits, crumbled

For the filling

450 g mascarpone cheese or any soft cheese

140 g icing sugar

120 g white chocolate melted

3 packets raspberry jelly (1 held for the top)

150 g raspberries, fresh or frozen

500 ml cream, softly whipped

To make the base melt the butter and add to the crumbled biscuit. Spoon the mixture into a 25 mm loose bottomed tin and flatten down with a spoon until smooth. Leave to chill in the fridge for one hour.

Mix the cheese and the icing sugar in a bowl with an electric mixer. Melt the white chocolate and allow to cool a little. Dissolve two packets of jelly in warm water and allow to cool slightly. Add the raspberries and melted white chocolate to the cheese and stir. Add in the dissolved cooled jelly and mix well. Fold in the softly whipped cream and mix well. Spoon over the biscuit base and place in the fridge for 2 hours until set.

Dissolve the remaining packet of jelly and allow to cool. Once cool pour the jelly over the cheesecake and allow to set.

SWEET RECIPES

Apple Jelly

1.3 kg cooking apples or crab apples, coarsely cut with peels on

1.5 l water

450 g sugar per pint of strained juice

Clean sterilised jars will be required to store the jelly

In a large saucepan boil the apples in the water until soft. Pour this mix into a jelly bag made from muslin suspended over a bowl. Allow the mix to strain overnight gathering the juice in a bowl. Measure the collected juice and allow 450 g of sugar for every pint of juice collected.

In a saucepan bring the juice to the boil and add the sugar. Increase the heat and boil rapidly until the setting point has been reached. You will know when this has happened by conducting the 'saucer test' – put a little jelly on a saucer and leave for a few minutes, run your finger over the jelly and if you achieve a ripple effect on the jelly the setting point has been reached.

Remove from the heat and pour into clean sterilised jars.

STRAWBERRY AND RHUBARB CRUMBLE

For the crumble mix

225 G PLAIN FLOUR

55 G PORRIDGE OATS

25 G MIXED CHOPPED NUTS

75 G WHITE SUGAR

75 G BROWN SUGAR

1½ TSP BAKING POWDER

112 G MARGARINE

For the fruit mix

900 G RHUBARB, CHOPPED

450 G STRAWBERRIES

100 G SUGAR

Preheat the oven to 180°C. In a mixing bowl combine the flour, porridge oats, nuts, sugars and baking powder. Rub in the margarine until the mixture resembles breadcrumbs.

Place the rhubarb and strawberries into a 23 cm ovenproof dish and mix in the sugar. Cover evenly with the crumble mix and bake at 180°C for 30 minutes until nicely browned.

Serve with freshly whipped cream or ice cream.

CHEF'S TIP

For delicious variations use rhubarb and banana or apple and strawberry.

BOILED FRUIT CAKE

For first stage

200 G RAISINS

200 G CURRANTS

50 G GLACE CHERRIES

55 G CHOPPED WALNUTS OR CHOPPED PECANS

170 G SUGAR

110 G MARGARINE

1 TSP BREAD SODA

225 ML WATER

For second stage

225 G SIEVED PLAIN FLOUR

2 EGGS, BEATEN

2 TSP BAKING POWDER

1 TSP MIXED SPICE

This recipe comes from Sr Benedict's Canadian grandmother and should be made in two stages for a better flavoured cake.

Mix the ingredients for this first stage in a large saucepan, bring slowly to the boil and allow to boil for 5 minutes. Leave to stand overnight.

Preheat the oven to 170°C. Add to your mix the ingredients for the second stage and mix well. Spoon the cake mixture into a greased and lined 2 lb loaf tin and bake at 170°C for 1 hour and 10 minutes.

Allow to cool in the tin for 15 minutes before removing and turning onto a wire rack to cool completely.

GOOSEBERRY JAM

1.5 KG GOOSEBERRIES

475 ML WATER

1.5 KG SUGAR

Wash, top and tail the gooseberries. Place the gooseberries in a saucepan with the water and simmer for 30 minutes until reduced by about a third. Meanwhile gently heat the sugar in a pot on the cooker. Add the slightly warmed sugar to the gooseberry mix, bring to the boil and turn down the heat to simmer for 30 minutes until the setting point has been reached. You can check this by conducting the 'saucer test' – put a little jelly on a saucer and leave for a few minutes; run your finger over the jelly and if you achieve a ripple effect on the jelly the setting point has been reached. Sterilise six 450 g jars and lids by washing and turning upside down on a baking tray and placing in a heated oven for twenty minutes. Turn off the heat and remove the scum off the top of the jam before jarring. Use a jug to fill, lid and label at once.

CHEF'S TIP

Sometimes we are lucky enough to have elderflower cordial here at Kylemore, of which a few tablespoons could be added during the softening of the gooseberries to add another flavour.

FARMHOUSE FRUIT CAKE

250 G FLOUR

1 TSP MIXED SPICE

900 G MIXED DRIED FRUIT (SULTANAS, APRICOTS, PRUNES AND CRANBERRIES)

100 G CHERRIES

225 G BUTTER

200 G CASTER SUGAR

5 EGGS, BEATEN

125 G WALNUTS

Preheat oven to 140°C.

Line a 20 cm cake tin with greaseproof paper. Sieve the flour and spice into a bowl and combine with the mixed fruit and cherries. Cream the butter and sugar in a mixing bowl until light and fluffy. Add the beaten egg gradually to the mix, beating well between additions. Fold in the flour and fruit mix. Add in the walnuts and stir to mix together. Put the mix into the prepared tin and bake at 160°C for two hours. Test with a skewer to ensure the cake is cooked and cool before removing from the tin.

ROCKY ROAD

450 g milk chocolate

200 g digestive biscuits

2 packets smarties

1 packet marshmallows (if large cut up half of them into quarters)

1 packet mini white buttons

Melt the chocolate gently in a bowl over a saucepan of boiling water. Stir to ensure that all of the chocolate has melted, remove from the heat and add the digestive biscuits broken into quarters. Add one packet of the smarties and half the marshmallows, then stir to ensure everything is covered in chocolate. We use baking parchment on our tray because it makes it easier to turn out and cut into smaller squares once set. Spread the chocolate mix across a lined swiss roll tin, pressing down to remove any air bubbles. Decorate with the remaining marshmallows, smarties and buttons. Press these into the chocolate to ensure they stick and remain on your rocky road. Allow to set for at least 90 minutes in the fridge. Remove from the fridge for a few minutes before serving to bring them to room temperature for cutting and eating.

SWEET RECIPES

113

PEACH TRAY BAKE

250 G SELF-RAISING FLOUR

1 TSP BAKING POWDER

225 G CASTOR SUGAR

225 G SOFT BUTTER

50 ML MILK

4 EGGS

2 TRAYS OF FRESH PEACHES SLICED

Line a deep swiss roll tin with parchment paper. Sieve the flour and baking powder into a large bowl, then add in the castor sugar. Add in the butter, milk, eggs and mix. Mix in the sliced peaches and spoon into a lined tray and bake for 30–35 mins at 150°C.

CHEF'S TIP

This could be made with berries or pears or any combination of fruit.

SPICED APPLE AND WALNUT BREAD

245 G PLAIN FLOUR
160 G CASTER SUGAR
70 G WALNUTS, CHOPPED
1 TSP BAKING POWDER
½ TSP BREAD SODA
¼ TSP NUTMEG
1 TSP CINNAMON
½ TSP GINGER

½ TSP SALT
60 G DRIED CRANBERRIES
100 ML VEGETABLE OIL
100 ML PLAIN YOGHURT
2 EGGS
1 TSP VANILLA EXTRACT
1 LARGE APPLE, PEELED, CORED AND SHREDDED

Preheat the oven to 160°C and line a 2 lb loaf tin.

Mix all the dry ingredients together in a large bowl except the apple. Mix all the wet ingredients in a separate bowl, then add the wet ingredients to the dry ones and mix well. Fold in the shredded apple. Spoon the mixture into a lined 2 lb loaf tin and bake for 40–50 minutes.

CHEF'S TIP

Sprinkle some walnuts and cranberries on top to decorate.

BANANA AND WALNUT BREAD

230 G PLAIN FLOUR

1 TSP SALT

1 TSP BAKING POWDER

1 TSP CINNAMON

115 G CASTER SUGAR

1 EGG, BEATEN

85 G BUTTER, MELTED

1 TSP VANILLA ESSENCE

70 G WALNUTS

4 MEDIUM BANANAS, MASHED

Preheat oven to 180°C and prepare a 2lb loaf tin.

Peel and mash the bananas on a plate.

Sieve the flour, salt, baking powder and cinnamon into a mixing bowl, then add the caster sugar and mix.

Melt the butter and add to the beaten egg. Add in the vanilla essence.

Add the banana to the butter and egg mix, fold into the dry ingredients in the mixing bowl and stir to combine.

Add the walnuts and pour into the prepared tin and bake for 45 minutes in the centre of the oven.

SWEET GUINNESS BREAD

- 240 ml wholemeal flour
- 240 ml plain flour
- 120 ml butter
- ½ tsp bread soda
- 60 ml caster sugar
- 2 tbsp treacle
- 250 ml Guinness
- 170 ml buttermilk

Preheat the oven to 170°C. Put the flours, butter, bread soda and sugar in a mixer and mix well until butter is blended. Heat the treacle, add it to the Guinness and then add the mixture to the buttermilk. Slowly add the Guinness mixture into the flour mixture while continuing to mix together. Oil a 2 lb loaf tin and pour the bread mix into the tin. The bread mixture will be quite wet. Bake for 55 minutes at 170°C. Tip the bread out of the tin onto a wire rack to cool completely. Serve with lashings of real Irish butter.

CHEF'S TIP

Seeds or chopped nuts can be sprinkled on top to give the bread a healthy appearance.

SR KAROL'S SCONES

450 G PLAIN FLOUR

1 HEAPED TSP OF BAKING POWDER

1 HEAPED TSP OF BREAD SODA

PINCH OF SALT

112 G BUTTER OR MARGARINE

112 G SULTANAS

25 ML BUTTERMILK OR SOUR MILK

This recipe was handed down to Sr Karol from her mother.

Preheat the oven to 180°C.

Sieve the flour, baking powder, bread soda and salt into a mixing bowl. Rub in the butter and add the sultanas. Make a well in the centre and add in the milk, stirring to combine. Turn out onto a floured board and knead lightly. Roll out to a thickness of 25 mm and cut into rounds using a scone cutter. Lightly brush with a little milk and place on a greased baking tray. Place the tray in a preheated oven at 180°C for 20 minutes. Once cooked, turn out onto a wire tray and allow to cool slightly before eating. Beautiful served with Kylemore Strawberry or Raspberry Jam and freshly whipped cream.

SWEET RECIPES

CHRISTMAS RECIPES

A flavour of KYLEMORE ABBEY

CHRISTMAS RECIPES

The feast of the birth of Jesus is celebrated liturgically in our Monastic Church all through the Christmas season. Locals and visitors join the community, especially for the Christmas Carols service. Wonderfully bedecked Christmas trees, brightly lit fires and candlelight create a mystical atmosphere. The aromatic smells of Christmas abound as puddings, cranberry sauce, ham glaze, chutneys and mincemeat are prepared and as Christmas cakes and mince pies are baked. Beautifully crafted Christmas decorations adorn the Abbey for this most holy of celebrations that is a timeless memory in the making for those who visit Kylemore together with our neighbours and friends.

KYLEMORE CHRISTMAS CAKE

The fruit

55 g candied peel

55 g cut washed cherries

300 g raisins

300 g sultanas

80 g flaked almonds

juice and zest of 1 orange

10 ml brandy

The cake

200 g butter

200 g dark Barbados sugar

4 eggs

200 g plain flour

40 g self raising flour

40 g ground almonds

pinch of salt

3 tsp mixed spice

2 tsp ground cinnamon

1 tsp ground nutmeg

The night before you make the cake, mix together the fruit, flaked almonds, orange zest and rind and soak in the brandy.

Prepare a 20 cm round fruit cake tin and double layer with greaseproof paper. Preheat the oven to 130°C and place your shelf just below the middle of the oven.

Cream the butter until pale, then add the sugar and beat for 3 minutes. Whisk the eggs. Sieve together the flours, ground almonds, salt and spices. Transfer the butter mixture into a large mixing bowl then slowly add the whisked eggs and then fold in the flour mixture. Add the fruit, being careful to scrape the fruit bowl well – all the juice belongs to the cake.

Turn into the lined tin and hollow out the centre. Wet your hand well and pinch the fruit under the surface of the mix to stop it burning. Place in the oven for 2 hours 20 minutes. When cooked allow to cool for approximately 30 minutes and then splash brandy on top. When the cake is completely cold wrap it first in greaseproof paper, then in brown paper and finally in cling film.

ROYAL ICING

3 EGG WHITES

675 G ICING SUGAR SIFTED

1½ TSP GLYCERINE (AVAILABLE FROM CHEMISTS, THIS PREVENTS THE ICING FROM BECOMING HARD AND BRITTLE)

Place the egg whites in a spotlessly clean bowl. Whisk them for about two minutes until they are starting to foam. Add the icing sugar a little at a time while continuing to whisk at a low speed. Continue to add the sugar until the mixture is stiff and peaking, then whisk in the glycerine.

TO DECORATE YOUR CHRISTMAS CAKE

Cover the cake in a layer of marzipan. Leave for one day, then, using a palette knife, spread the icing over the marzipan layer and cover the sides and top. Smooth over and add your choice of decoration. Leave to dry for 24 hours.

CHRISTMAS MINCEMEAT

450 G COOKING APPLES, PEELED, CORED AND FINELY CHOPPED

225 G SUET, SHREDDED

340 G RAISINS

225 G SULTANAS

225 G WHOLE MIXED PEEL, FINELY CHOPPED

340 G SOFT DARK BROWN SUGAR

GRATED RIND AND JUICE OF 2 ORANGES AND 2 LEMONS

55 G WHOLE ALMONDS, CHOPPED

4 TSP MIXED SPICE

½ TSP CINNAMON

½ A NUTMEG, GRATED

15 ML BRANDY

Mix all the ingredients together, except the brandy, in a large bowl. Cover and leave for 12 hours. Place the mix, loosely covered with foil, in a cool heated oven 120°C for 3 hours mixing occasionally. Remove from the oven and allow to cool. When the mix is cold, stir in the brandy and pour into the clean sterilised jars.

CHEF'S TIP

Use for your mince pies or for a larger tart. We sometimes use this in our Bakewell Tart instead of raspberry jam.

KYLEMORE LIQUEUR CREAM CUSTARD

250 ML CREAM

250 ML KYLEMORE ABBEY IRISH COUNTRY CREAM

4 TSP SUGAR

4 EGGS

2 TSP CORNFLOUR

Beat all the ingredients together in a saucepan and cook over a very low heat until it thickens, beating all the time. Serve warm with Kylemore Abbey Christmas Pudding.

CHEF'S TIP

Mix the cornflour into a small amount of cream before adding to the rest of the ingredients to avoid lumps. Remember to stir continuously over a low heat. Liqueur cream is ready when it coats the back of the wooden spoon. This liqueur cream recipe is derived from a recipe given to our community from Ypres.

CHRISTMAS RECIPES

KYLEMORE ABBEY CHRISTMAS PUDDING

1.2 KG MIXED DRIED FRUIT (WE USE A MIX OF SULTANAS, RAISINS, CURRANTS AND MIXED PEEL)

110 G GLACÉ CHERRIES

450 G BROWN SUGAR

450 G BREADCRUMBS

1 TSP CINNAMON

1 TSP MIXED SPICE

½ TSP NUTMEG

170 G SELF-RAISING FLOUR

170 G VEGETABLE SUET

170 G NIBBED ALMONDS

1 CARROT, PEELED AND GRATED

1 COOKING APPLE, PEELED AND GRATED

2 TBSP TREACLE

6 EGGS, BEATEN

GRATED RIND AND JUICE OF 1 LEMON AND 1 ORANGE

175 ML WHISKEY

280 ML STOUT (YOU MAY NEED A LITTLE MORE)

This quantity will make three 2 lb Christmas puddings.

Mix all of the dry ingredients together. Add the grated carrot and apple and mix. Mix together the eggs, lemon and orange rind and juice, treacle, whiskey and stout. Add this to pudding mixture. Leave to stand overnight. The following day fill pudding bowls to within about 3 cm of the rim. Cover the mix with a lid or alternatively with 2 layers of greaseproof paper and tie down the sides. Steam for 6 hours in a saucepan of simmering water, taking care that no water enters the pudding bowl.

Serve warm with Kylemore Liqueur Cream Custard.

CHEF'S TIP

Pour some brandy over your warm pudding just before serving and set alight for a magical Christmas effect.

CHRISTMAS RECIPES

FRANGIPANE MINCE PIES

For the base

125 G FLOUR

75 G BUTTER SOFTENED

50 G SUGAR

330 G MINCEMEAT

30 G FLAKED ALMONDS

For the frangipane

100 G BUTTER

100 G CASTER SUGAR

2 EGGS

100 G GROUND ALMONDS

Preheat your oven to 150°C and grease your 12-piece mince pie tray. Using a mixer make the base by combining the the flour, butter and sugar until they form a stiff dough. Roll out and line the bottom of the pie tray.

For the frangipane mix, cream the butter and sugar together in a mixing bowl until light and creamy. Beat in the eggs a little at a time to prevent curdling. Fold in the ground almonds and mix gently to make your frangipane mix.

Spread the mincemeat mix over the shortbread base evenly, spoon the frangipane mix over and smooth to the edge. Sprinkle with the flaked almonds. Bake for 45 minutes at 150°C.

CHRISTMAS RECIPES

131